KU-520-536

OLYSLAGER AUTO LIBRARY

Passenger Vehicles 1893-1940

compiled by the OLYSLAGER ORGANISATION
research by Denis N. Miller
edited by Bart H. Vanderveen

FREDERICK WARNE & Co Ltd
London and New York

THE OLYSLAGER AUTO LIBRARY

This book is one of a growing range of titles on major transport subjects.
Titles published so far include:

The Jeep
Half-Tracks
Scammell Vehicles
Fire-Fighting Vehicles
Earth-Moving Vehicles
Wreckers and Recovery Vehicles
Passenger Vehicles
Fairground and Circus Transport

American Cars of the 1930s
American Cars of the 1940s
American Cars of the 1950s

British Cars of the Early Thirties
British Cars of the Late Thirties

HERTFORDSHIRE
COUNTY LIBRARY

629.2223 30904

6145616

Copyright © Olyslager Organisation BV 1973

Library of Congress Catalog Card No 73-80248

ISBN 0 7232 1726 2

Filmset and printed in Great Britain
by BAS Printers Limited, Wallop, Hampshire

460·473

INTRODUCTION

To many of us the passenger road vehicle is merely a method of travelling to and from work, visiting relatives, or even going on holiday. It is convenient (sometimes) and that is all. To others it holds a fascination of its own. The study of its development, from the earliest horse-drawn types to the latest gas turbine, propane gas and electrically-propelled designs, is a complex subject and one which could never be tackled in full by any historian, no matter how keen.

In this volume we have reproduced many rare and hitherto unpublished photographs, illustrating as near as possible the development of the bus and coach up to 1940, including prototypes, experimental designs and important breakthroughs from many parts of the world.

Although it was a Frenchman who instigated the first regular passenger service by road, the philosopher Blaise Pascal in 1662 offered a complete coach hire system (later banned by government decree!), it was left to British and German manufacturers (notably Daimler, Magirus, Leyland and Thornycroft) to develop the road-going passenger vehicle from its dubious horse-drawn ancestry to its modern streamlined image of ultra-efficiency.

It is intriguing to note how the designs of 1940 evolved from those of 1900. The earliest types were invariably 'one-offs', based on truck-type chassis, frequently incorporating former horsebus bodies (both single- and double-decked) or bodies constructed along very similar lines.

Later, for ease of access, the low-loading chassis designed specifically for passenger operation made its appearance, increased and more effective weatherproofing was added (such as canvas shields for the use of upper deck passengers in wet weather) and a greater emphasis placed upon safety. By the late Twenties many upper saloons were fully enclosed, although some types continued to feature open rear staircases right up to the mid-Thirties.

Double-deck models were, with relatively few exceptions, a British phenomenon. Six-wheeled designs, similarly, were largely confined to the British Isles, Germany and certain American states. Semi-trailer applications could be found on the continent of Europe and in areas where immense distances between conurbations were commonplace.

Our research tells us that the war years (1940–45) were principally a period of stagnation in the passenger road transportation field, with many manufacturing facilities turned over to the production of wartime necessities such as weapons, ammunition, military vehicles, aircraft and the like. Thus, 1940 is where we complete this first survey, which is arranged by vehicle make, in alphabetical order.

Piet Olyslager MSIA, MSAE, KIVI

3A : As a summer tourist attraction, Polperro, Cornwall, has its own horsebus service.
3B : A rare design of 'stagecoach', with a steam engine at front and rear, each powering one of the axles, appeared in the USA in 1893.
3C : This battery-operated 3-wheeler with semi-trailer provided a hotel bus service in Lucerne, Switzerland, some years ago.

3A

3B

3C

AEC

4A: In 1910 the first examples of the immortal AEC/LGOC B-Type bus were produced. When war broke out in 1914 about 3000 were in service and many were subsequently used as troop carriers by the British Forces in France and Belgium. Shown are some of these on the quayside at Boulogne, en route for the front.

4B: The crew of LA 9839 taking a break in rural setting outside 'The Hare' at Brooks Hill, Harrow Weald.

4C: The K-Type, introduced in August 1919, was the first British 'forward-control' passenger model to attain quantity production and the first with transverse seating in the lower saloon.

4B   AEC

4A   AEC

4C   AEC

5A: Announced in 1929, the AEC 'Regal' single-deck model was destined to revolutionize the British coaching industry. The 'all weather coach', with roll-back roof covering, was typical of the early Thirties when this example was delivered to the East Surrey Traction Company.
5B: F. W. Plaxton's B3 passenger body had a front entrance and 37 seats. It was designed for bus operation despite the coach styling and sliding passenger door. The chassis was a later version of the AEC 'Regal'.
5C: The first trolleybuses acquired by London United Tramways, in 1931, were AEC 663T types with 56-seat rear-entrance Union Construction Co bodies. Chassis were similar to the 'Renown' motor bus but with the 80-hp traction motor hidden under the bonnet!

5B AEC

5A AEC

5C AEC

AEC

6 : 262 vehicles, using the 'Renown' chassis, were supplied to London General in 1932. They were popularly known as 'Bluebird LT's, some with heavy oil and others with petrol engines.

7A : AEC Q5, delivered in 1934, was London Transport's fourth side-engined (petrol) double-decker and the second of this type to have a centre entrance. It was the seventeenth double-deck 'Q' to be built. Bodywork was by Weymann.

7B : VH 6218 (*c.* 1934) was one of six ex-Huddersfield AEC 'Regents' purchased by Bournemouth Corporation in 1945. Within two years the original body had been removed, the chassis shortened and an over-head inspection tower added, as shown here.

7C : London's X4 Class trolleybus, delivered in 1936, was based on the standard AEC 663T 'Renown' type chassis. An unusual feature of this series, however, was the front exit with jack-knife doors.

7A AEC

7B AEC

7C AEC

ALBION

ALBION

9A Albion

9B Albion

8 : Albion Motors' Model 24, a 20-seat design, was one of a range of small-capacity machines favoured by many Scottish operators who had to contend with sparsely populated rural routes. The Model 24 was in production during 1923—32. Specimen shown was delivered in May 1925.

9A : In 1925 this Albion Model 26 accomplished a non-stop run from Glasgow, round Eros in Piccadilly, London, and back to Glasgow in just over 24 hours. Seating capacity was 36. Model 26 production period was 1925—33.

9B : The Albion Model 28 'Viking Six' was offered during 1926—32 in normal- or forward-control forms. This 30-seat forward-control version was delivered to Messrs Baillie Bros Ltd in Glasgow in 1931.

9C : The Albion CX.19 'Venturer', a 56-seat double-deck machine, appeared in 1938. The Sydney Transport Board, New South Wales, ran a considerable fleet of these for many years, the majority having sliding windows in the upper saloon.

9C Albion

ASSOCIATED DAIMLER, BAT

10A: LS6 (London Six) in the LGOC fleet was
an Associated Daimler (ADC) Model 802,
unique in that it was the only chassis of this
type to carry a single-deck body—and only a
34-seater at that. 1927.

10B: The BAT, built in London and Bristol by
Messrs Harris & Hasell Ltd in 1930 and 1931,
was a real rarity, intended principally for the
rural operator. The British market, however,
was already saturated with vehicles of this
class, many being the products of well
established manufacturers. Thus, the BAT
soon sank into obscurity. This specimen was
in service with St Albans District Motor
Services.

10A   Associated Daimler

10B   BAT

11A: Smallest passenger model in the pre-war LPTB fleet was a 14-seat machine produced by Bean Cars Ltd, Dudley, Worcs. in 1930. Three such vehicles were acquired from Messrs F. C. Owen, of Windsor, upon the unification of services in 1933.

11B: Vauxhall Motors introduced their first Bedford 2-ton coach chassis in mid-1931. Until 1934 there were two models, both with the 26.3 HP 6-cyl. OHV engine: Model WHB with 131-inch wheelbase (Chassis Nos. 100001-100035) and WLB with 157-inch wheelbase (108001-109562). During 1934–35 there was a slightly modified WLB (109801-110133), an example of which is shown here with Duple 20-seater bodywork.

11C: In 1935 Vauxhall announced the new 3-ton 167-inch wheelbase semi-FC Bedford Model WTB chassis, intended for operation with 26-seater bodywork. Until 1938 (Chassis Nos. 110201-112445) the WTB had the earlier 26.3 HP power unit but during 1938–39 (1001-20287) a 28 HP engine was used. Both were OHV Sixes, with $3\frac{5}{16} \times 3\frac{3}{4}$ inch and $3\frac{3}{8} \times 4\frac{1}{8}$ inch bore and stroke respectively.

11B Bedford

11A Bean

11C Bedford

BENZ

12 : Carl Benz' first motor bus, in 1895, was this *Hotelwagen-Omnibus* for eight passengers. Basically a motorized carriage, it had a 5 HP engine, located just ahead of the back axle.

13A : Relatively uncommon outside France, this 'cab-over-engine' Berliet 18CV Model CAT was operated by the Bristol Tramways & General Electric Co Ltd *c.* 1911. Exit from the lower saloon was accomplished via steps at the forward end of the body.

13B : The Model CB Berliet was also of 1911 vintage but of normal control design. This was a single-deck model with strengthened roof and additional upper deck seating encased within a canvas shroud ; it operated in Oran.

13C : Berliet trucks and buses were often propelled by producer gas, as exemplified by this pneumatic-tyred chain-drive model of the Twenties.

13B   Berliet

13A   Berliet

13C   Berliet

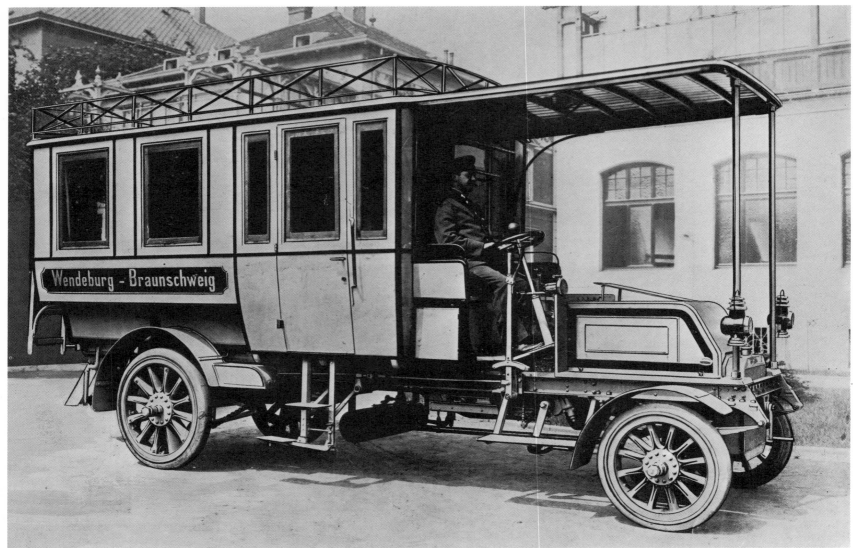

Wendeburg - Braunschweig

14: First in a long line of passenger types sold under the Büssing name left the Braunschweig, Germany, plant in June 1904. The body of this machine comprised three sections—rear saloon, central saloon and driving area. Similar Büssing chassis were licence-produced in Britain, by Straker-Squire.

15A: Leipzig took delivery of a fleet of Büssing double-deckers in 1913.
In common with major British types of this period, these were of 'bonneted' (normal-control) layout with a 'live' rear axle.

15B: The Twenties saw the large-scale intro-duction of six-wheeled passenger models. These Büssing *Dreiachs-Omnibusse* of the Hamburger Hochbahn were delivered in 1923, incorporating rear entrance doors and lengthwise seating.

15C: The underfloor-engined Büssing-NAG *Dreiachser* of 1939 ran on single tyres and was of dual entrance/exit layout. The low step height was also an interesting feature. Engine was a 140-bhp Model UD6 six-cylinder. This vehicle operated in Hanover.

15B   Büssing

15A   Büssing

15C   Büssing-NAG

CEDES-STOLL

16 : A pioneer of trolleybus operation was the Aberdare UDC who, on 13 January 1914, inaugurated a Cedes-Stoll system devised by the Mercedes Stoll Electric Traction Company. This system comprised eight cars with traction motors by Johnson & Phillips, of Charlton, London.

17A : Also in 1914, experiments were carried out in Hove, Sussex, with the Cedes-Stoll system. The 5½-ton double-deck machine with 33-seat Christopher Dodson body was, however, considered by many to be unsafe and the entire system was abandoned the following year.

17B : Chevrolet Model LQ, produced in the UK before General Motors'

introduction of the British-designed Vauxhall-built Bedford WHB, with 14-seat bodywork intended for rural operation. Example shown was operated by Harwood's, a Surrey 'independent' before the formation of the LPTB.

17C : An interesting rival of the petrol-engined passenger vehicle at the turn of the century was the steam bus. Thomas Clarkson, an inventor, of Chelmsford, Essex, designed and built a number of machines of this type as early as 1903. Note the 'wrap-round' wind-screen and full-width driver's bench seat.

17A   Cedes-Stoll

17B   Chevrolet

17C   Clarkson

COMMER

1289

18 : Off to a football match Australian style—some sixty years ago ! Despite the park bench type seating secured to this Commer's flat body, remarkably few of the 31 passengers appear to be using this as it was intended.

19A : Known affectionately as 'The Yellow Peril', this surviving Commer shooting brake of 1913 was based on a similar chassis to the vehicle shown opposite. Unusual features included a pre-selector transmission, aluminium oil bath for the chain final drive and transmission braking.

19B : Reported to be of approximately 1919 vintage, this charabanc was owned by Messrs Toppings, of Liverpool. It could seat some thirty people and was provided with a full-length collapsible hood.

19C : The 'Avenger' appeared in 1930 as a 32-seat single-deck or 50-seat double-deck bus. It was powered by a 105-bhp 6-cylinder engine. Designated NF6, this was the heaviest Commer passenger model produced up to World War II.

19B Commer

19A Commer

19C Commer

20: The 1½-ton Commer 'Raider' was not originally intended for use as a passenger model, but many were built as special ambulance chassis and could be fitted out as small buses or shooting brakes. In 1934 this shooting brake cost a mere £536, including such extras as Triplex glass and aluminium step mats.

21A Commer

21A: Commer's PNF-Series was introduced in 1936, powered by any one of a range of 6-cylinder petrol engines and available with seating capacities of between 20 and 26. For overseas use, however, these seating capacities were not rigidly adhered to. This African example, for instance, could carry 36 passengers albeit in somewhat cramped conditions. Note the dual entrance/exit design, lack of window glass and the provision of roll-down side canvas for passenger protection in poor weather.

21B: The PLNF5 was a forward-control version of the Commer PNF-Series, introduced in 1938 and designed to carry 26 passengers. Note the richly embellished bodywork and generally streamlined styling.

21B Commer

CROSSLEY

22 : When the newly formed LPTB took over Middlesex operator Filkins & Ainsworth in November 1933, four attractive little Crossley buses passed into London Transport's Country Area fleet. All were one man-operated vehicles, and at least two had a front entrance and rear exit!

23A : This German Daimler post-bus of 1906 was powered by a 28 HP 4-cylinder engine driving a 'live' rear axle. Note the curtained windows and ladder access to the roof luggage area. It operated in Bavaria.

23B : The East Surrey Traction Co experimented with a British Daimler demonstration model for a short time before World War I, presumably to obtain comparative data against their existing fleet.

23C : In 1934 Birmingham Corporation Transport took delivery of a batch of Daimler COG5 double-deck models with 50-seat bodies by the Birmingham Railway Carriage & Wagon Company. No. 166 was observed, minus upper saloon, in Nicosia, Cyprus, in May 1955.

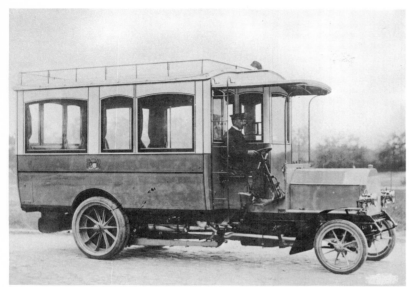

23A   Daimler (D)

23B   Daimler (GB)

23C   Daimler (GB)

DENNIS

24 : Typical of its kind, this Dennis 40 HP 29-seater *Char-à-Bancs* was operated by the Mourne Mountains Touring Co Ltd of Rostrevor, Northern Ireland. Finished in aluminium it had six doors, all on the left-hand side. The French term *Char-à-Bancs* (plural) indicated a bus body design with folding top and transverse bench-type seats. The British adopted this term, albeit usually modified to 'charabanc' (one word, singular). 'Toast-rack' was a popular British word for open-sided charabancs, i.e. without any doors.

25A : From 1927 the H-Series double-decker replaced the Dennis Company's 4-ton model. Some of the first deliveries, to the LGOC, had open-top bodies but those delivered to a London independent operator, Ambassador Omnibus Company, of N19, had enclosed saloons with an open staircase at the rear, as illustrated.

25B : The Dennis 'Dart' was a 6-cylinder version of its predecessor, the GL-Series, resembling this in size and layout. The LGOC purchased a small fleet of 'Darts' in 1931, fitting them with 20-seat front-entrance bus bodies for one-man-operation.

25C : This photograph, taken at Taunton, Somerset, in 1947, shows two Dennis's and a Bristol operated by the Western National Omnibus Company at that time. In the foreground is a 1932 'Lancet I' with 32-seat Beadle body and in the middle a 1935 ECW-bodied 'Mace', more common with a full-front body.

25A   Dennis

25B   Dennis

25C   Dennis

FIAT

26: Between 1911 and 1921 Fiat of Italy offered a *Char-à-Bancs* design based on their 2F chassis. This was powered by a 20-hp engine and had a seating capacity of 10 to 12. Note the disc wheels, access ladder to roof rack and roll-down canvas side blinds.

27A: Fiat introduced the 18 BL omnibus in 1914, based on a 38-hp chassis. Carrying capacity was 20 to 24 persons. Note the post box on the front left-hand side.

27B: In 1937 the Fiat 656 RNL was introduced for city use. This could carry 76 passengers, the majority standing, and was intended for use as a commuter bus for short-distance peak hour travel. Production continued until 1939, all examples being powered by a 115-bhp 6-cylinder diesel engine.

27C: The single-deck trolleybus has never been a popular machine in the British Isles except, perhaps, during the Twenties and during the early years of experimental operation—but on the Continent it remains popular even today. This FN/CED front-entrance rear-exit design was constructed by Fabrique Nationale d'Armes de Guerre (now Fabrique Nationale Herstal), a Belgian company specializing in the construction of military equipment. This machine appeared in 1933.

27B   Fiat

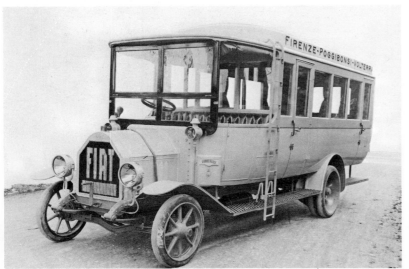

27A   Fiat

27C   FN/CED

FODEN

28 : E. Foden, Sons & Co Ltd constructed a single steam bus in 1914, using their 'overtype' wagon (i.e. with loco type front end). There were no restrictions on overhang in those days and passenger access was, apparently, a secondary consideration !

29A : Even in those early days certain rail routes in the UK were uneconomical for full-sized trains to operate. Thus, the light-weight small-capacity railcar train was considered to be the answer. This outfit comprised two Ford Model Ts, back-to-back, with an additional carriage between them. The Model T Ford was one of the most famous chassis of all time and one of the most ubiquitous.

29B : Originally delivered to the Skylark Motor Coach Co Ltd, of London, W1, this Gilford 166SD with Duple coachwork was one of a batch acquired by Green Line, the LGOC subsidiary, in February 1932. The 166SD was introduced in 1928, powered by a new 6-cylinder American-built Lycoming petrol engine.

29A Ford

29B Gilford

GMC, GRAHAM BROS

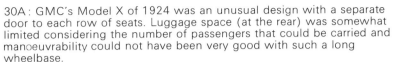

30A: GMC's Model X of 1924 was an unusual design with a separate door to each row of seats. Luggage space (at the rear) was somewhat limited considering the number of passengers that could be carried and manoeuvrability could not have been very good with such a long wheelbase.

30B: The Cannery-Ghirardelli Square Omnibus Company continues to operate some *c.* 1925 GMC Model Z-230 open-top double-deck vehicles for sightseeing and as a tourist attraction. Each vehicle has an open rear staircase, enclosed driver's compartment and windshield for the upper deck.

30C: A New York operator, the Fifth Avenue Coach Co, founded in 1885, introduced a fleet of underfloor-engined maximum-capacity double-deck machines based on the GMC Model 720 chassis in 1936. Because of their size these vehicles were dubbed 'Queen Marys'.

30D: Photographed in Canberra, Australia, this American Graham Bros bus, based on Dodge Bros chassis, was ruggedly constructed to tackle the numerous 'bush' roads encountered in that country. Access to the luggage rack was via a rear ladder. Curtains at the windows were both for sleeping purposes and to keep out the scorching sun.

30A   GMC

30B   GMC

30C   GMC

30D   Graham Bros

GUY

31A: In 1926 Guy Motors Ltd, of Wolver-hampton, announced their first trolleybus—a revolutionary design incorporating high capacity (60 passengers), three axles and pneumatic tyres (believed to have been the first trolleybus to run on pneumatics anywhere in the world). Wolverhampton Corporation was the first operator to take delivery of the new machine, the BTX, and the first to convert its trolleybus fleet to this type and thus eradicate the old tramway image.

31B: Towards the end of 1933 Guy introduced its 'Wolf' and 'Vixen' small-capacity passenger models. Of these, those owned by the Llandudno UDC were perhaps the best known, being based on the CF20 chassis. The open-sided Waveney bodies each seated 20 persons.

31A Guy

31B Guy

HISPANO-SUIZA, INTERNATIONAL, KARRIER

32A   Hispano-Suiza

32C   Karrier

32B   International

32A: S. A. Hispano-Suiza, of Barcelona, Spain, designed and built both goods and passenger models from 1927 until the Forties. One elderly model (*c*.1934 vintage) was still running in 1967 and is seen here.

32B: For the UK market the American-controlled International Harvester Co of Great Britain Ltd offered two passenger types during the Twenties —the 4-cylinder SL for 18-seater bodies and the 6-cylinder SL.36 for 20-seaters. This example carried bodywork by Strachan & Brown Ltd.

32C: One of the earliest Karrier passenger models built by Clayton & Co (Huddersfield) Ltd (later Karrier Motors Ltd) was this 20-passenger A-Type of about 1912. It was chain driven and of the cab-over-engine layout, a popular configuration at that time.

33A: Another Karrier of about this time was the PB60 charabanc with seating for 18 passengers. This was of completely different layout to the A-Type, being of normal-control layout with double running boards, doors to each row of seats and collapsible hood.

33B: Only three examples of the Karrier 'Road-Railer' were built. The prototype (a forward-control 'Chaser' 26-seat model for the LMS) was followed by a goods version and finally this normal-control design for use on a narrow-gauge track in the Netherlands. This vehicle was delivered in 1930 to the Rotterdam Tramways Company.

33C: One of the more popular Continental passenger models imported into the UK during the Twenties and Thirties was the Italian Lancia. The 'Pentaiota', introduced at the 1925 Commercial Motor Show and seen here in the livery of Messrs Lewis, of Watford, Herts, had accommodation for up to 30 passengers.

33B Karrier

33A Karrier

33C Lancia

LEYLAND

34: In 1900 the Lancashire Steam Motor Co (later Leyland Motors Ltd) supplied a prototype steam bus to the Dundee Motor Omnibus Company. Mounted on Leyland's prize-winning wagon chassis of 1898, the bodywork was constructed to carry 18 passengers. Roof-mounted condensers made it unnecessary to carry great quantities of water.

35A: Early Leyland internal combustion-engined passenger models continued to bear the manufacturing plate of the Lancashire Steam Motor Co, mounted on the radiator stack. This was the single-deck variant of the Company's live-axle (shaft-drive) design of c. 1912.

35B: During the Twenties the *Char-à-Bancs* (or: charabanc) was very popular for passenger transport. They were built on ex-WD or new chassis of numerous makes. Illustrated is a smart specimen on a 1920s Leyland truck chassis with solid rear tyres and pneumatics at front. Legal speed limit being 12 mph, weather protection was not too important, although a full-length folding canvas hood was provided to keep the rain out (or at least most of it!). The *Char-à-Bancs* was used mainly for outings, day-trips to seaside resorts, and the like.

35C: The 4-wheeled 'Titan' double-deck passenger model, introduced at the 1927 Commercial Motor Show, introduced for the first time three important features in a British passenger model—a 6-cylinder engine, low frame height and vacuum brakes. This 1935 model had a 56-seat body by the Eastern Counties Omnibus Co Ltd (now ECW Ltd).

35A Leyland

35B Leyland

35C Leyland

LEYLAND

36A: Leyland Tiger of 1930, operated by the United Automobile Services of Norfolk and featuring an unusual design of sunshine roof.
36B: Whilst the 6-wheeled AEC 'Renown' enjoyed comparative popularity, the Leyland equivalent, known as the 'Titanic', was a rare piece of machinery. Doncaster Corporation received most of these. This specimen, No. 72, was delivered in 1936 with a 60-seat body by Charles H. Roe Ltd.

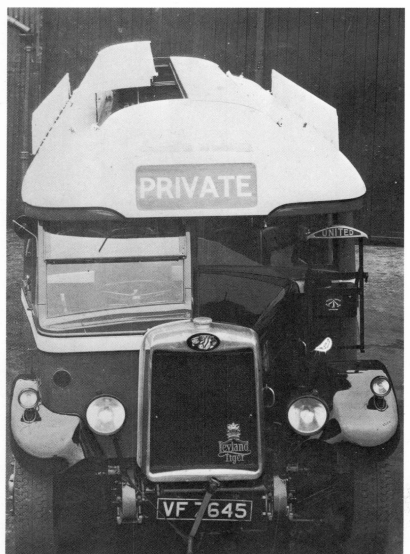

36A Leyland

36B Leyland

LEYLAND

37A: Although resembling the 'Titanic' in layout, this express coach in the ownership of the City Coach Company was, in fact, based on a trailing axle derivation of the Leyland 'Tiger', designated TS7T. A fleet of these was delivered to City c. 1935/6, some with 39 and others with 43 seats.

37B: The Leyland 'Gnu' 6-wheeler of 1938 was a twin-steer model designated Model TEP1 or TEC2. A similar machine, but with under-floor engine, was known as the 'Panda'; but whilst eight 'Gnu' chassis were built only one 'Panda' saw the light of day. The last TEP1 (with 40-seat centre-entrance Duple body) was delivered to the City Coach Co, of London, who subsequently received all five examples of the 39-seat TEC2.

37C: Following closely the twin-steer layout of the 'Gnu', a single all-Leyland chassisless trolleybus was purchased by the LPTB in September 1939. This had been a Leyland Motors demonstrator (hence the Lancs registration) and despite lengthwise seats at the forward end of the lower saloon seated the usual 70 passengers. It was disposed of in May 1955.

37A   Leyland

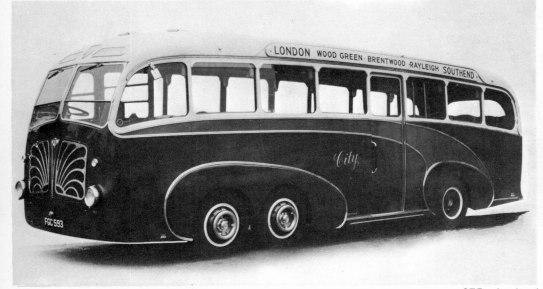

37B   Leyland

37C   Leyland

MACK

38 : The first motor bus produced by a US manufacturer was also the first successful Mack, built in 1900. It was a 20-seater with revolutionary (for the USA) steering wheel instead of the generally accepted tiller steering arrangement.

39A : Even in 1927 German postal buses were little different from those of the previous decade. This Magirus was of the convertible 'all weather' type with smartly contoured bodywork. Note the similarity to British charabancs of the period.

39B : Five years earlier, another German manufacturer—MAN—was offering fully-enclosed designs such as this. Designed principally for use as a touring coach or stage carriage vehicle, this featured a separate driver's compartment and a roof rack for bulky luggage. Specimen shown was supplied to the City of Nuremberg in 1922.

39C : Bearing a striking resemblance to GMC's Model X of 1924 (Fig. 30A), an unusual MAN design, also of 1924, was of shorter wheel-base resulting in an increased rear overhang.

39A Magirus

39B MAN

39C MAN

MANN

40: In 1917 this was the latest in demountable body systems! The availability of this Mann 'overtype' wagon was exploited to the full— during the week it carried general goods and at the weekend private parties. It would appear that the rearmost passengers could only alight with the aid of a set of portable steps, although some charabancs featured a centre aisle.

MARIENFELDER (DAIMLER), MARMON-HERRINGTON

41A: The Marienfelder was a relatively shortlived name in the vehicle manufacturing business. It was, in fact, the name given to products of the Daimler Company's Berlin Marienfelder plant. This 1903 model bore some similarity to Daimler's 1898 design, with the exception of the steering column (the early design was tiller-steered) and other minor refinements.

41B: One of Daimler's earliest post buses left the Marienfelder works in 1905. This was delivered to the Königlich-Bayerischen-Post and was unusual in that it featured a 'convertible' style body.

41C: An impressive Marmon-Herrington Model THD 315-6 six-wheel-drive tractor unit was acquired in 1932 (the year after Marmon-Herrington commenced truck manufacture) for use on the famed Nairn Bros' desert service in the Middle East, principally between Baghdad and Damascus. The luxuriously appointed air-conditioned semi-trailer could carry up to 40 passengers in comfort and the entire outfit was 75 ft in length and weighed nearly 30 tons.

41A Marienfelder

41B Marienfelder

41C Marmon-Herrington

MERCEDES-BENZ, MORRIS-COMMERCIAL

42: The Maudslay Motor Co's Model SF40, later re-named the 'Magna', was considerably ahead of its time when introduced in 1935. Most important feature was the set-back front axle, permitting the use of a full front entrance. Despite this, a greater percentage were supplied with centre-entrance coachwork exemplified by this Duple design for Messrs C. G. Lewis in 1936.

43A: By 1933 design of the German postal bus had improved considerably. Daimler-Benz announced the Mercedes-Benz Model LO2000 at about this time, this machine being designed specifically for passenger operation and yet incorporating many of the rugged features so familiar on the Company's trucks. The roof rack with ladder access was retained.

43B: The East Surrey Traction Co took delivery of six Morris-Commercial 'Viceroy' 20-seaters in 1931. Specification was close to that of the Dennis 'Dart', favoured by other operators with rural or semi-rural routes, both machines being ideally suited to the narrow lanes of the English countryside.

43C: In a bid to support local industry, Birmingham Corporation Transport purchased three Morris-Commercial 'Imperial' double-deck buses on an experimental basis in 1933. Each carried a different make of body, this being the third, with 48-seat coachwork by the Gloucester Carriage & Wagon Works. Later, it was adapted to seat 54 people.

43B Morris-Commercial

43C Morris-Commercial

43A Mercedes-Benz

44 : The Northern General Transport Co Ltd was one of only a handful of British operators to produce their own vehicles. In 1933 the then Chief Engineer, Mr. G. W. Hayter, drew up plans for the SE6 (side-engined 6-wheeler) and a prototype was assembled. Thirty-five examples were eventually constructed (all at AEC's Southall works), that shown being one of a batch of six with forward-entrance luxury coach bodies, seating 28 persons, produced in 1935.

45A : A 2-axle version of the SE6 appeared in 1936, designated the SE4. CPT 921, with its English Electric body, was typical of later production. Unlike the SE6, which had an American Hercules petrol engine, the SE4 was powered by an AEC diesel unit.

45B : Towards the end of World War II this dual entrance/exit French Panhard of mid-Thirties vintage was typical of the many thousands of assorted commercial and passenger vehicles impressed by the German forces. While some of their comrades remain on the vehicle's roof other Nazi soldiers attempt to manhandle the Panhard out of soft ground.

45C : The transport authorities of Prague, Czechoslovakia, took delivery of two special sight-seeing buses, based on tandem-drive Praga TOV chassis, in 1939. Operated by the City Traffic Enterprise, each was powered by a 6-cylinder petrol engine of 120 bhp driving through a 4-speed transmission. Note the gracious lines of front end and coachwork.

45B Panhard

45A NGT

45C Praga

DEPOT

RAILLESS, RAPID

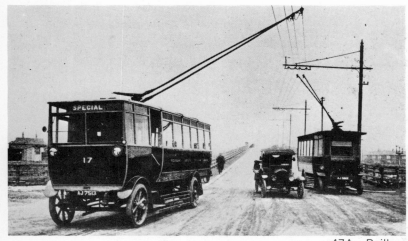

47A Railless

47C Rapid

47B Railless

46: Railless, a division of the Short Bros coachbuilding concern, specialized in the design and manufacture of trolleybuses. One of their most unusual designs was this ungainly machine supplied to Leeds City Transport in September 1921. Like many Railless designs, it was largely unsuccessful and was withdrawn from service after five years.

47A: One of the first trolleybus systems to be inaugurated in the UK after World War I was that of the Teesside Railless Traction Co. Overhead equipment was by Clough Smith and 'cars' by Railless, each featuring two 23-hp motors driving direct to the rear wheels.

47B: Birmingham's Railless vehicles, purchased for experimental operation on the Nechalls route in 1922, carried 51-seat Roe bodies. Twelve were supplied, each with a totally enclosed driver's cab, covered roof and open rear staircase.

47C: In 1909 the Rapid Motor Vehicle Co of Pontiac, Michigan, was acquired by General Motors. One of the last models to be sold under the Rapid name was a light 30-hp bus with longitudinal seating. Note the rolled-up side curtains which could be unfurled to provide added weather protection.

RENARD, RENAULT

48A : One of the more interesting exhibits at the Franco-British Exhibition, London, in 1908, was the Renard Road Train, designed by Colonel Renard, a French engineer, in 1902/03. Each of the six-wheeled wagons carried its own drive shaft and differential, all being coupled together with the drive transmitted from the rear axle of the tractor unit. Each wagon's centre axle was powered: Daimler in Coventry acquired exclusive British rights in 1907 and commenced production in 1908, but although some road trains were supplied to Australia, Canada, South Africa, the USA and several other countries, they were not successful and vanished for good at the time of the first World War.

48B : Renault charabanc in Reigate, Surrey, c. 1926. Note the fares : Reigate—Redhill three pence, London return six shillings. Like other contemporary Renaults it had a dash-mounted radiator.

48A   Renard

48B   Renault

49A   Reo

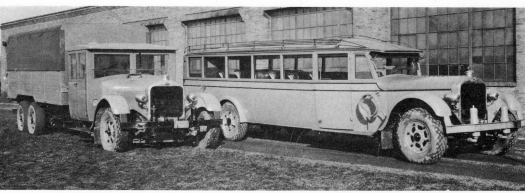

49B   Safeway

49C   Scania-Vabis

49A: Reo in the USA introduced their highly successful 'Speedwagon' in 1924. This 4-cylinder model could carry 20 seated passengers, ideal for one man-operated rural services. Production continued until 1931. Reo was founded by Ransom E. Olds after he left his earlier enterprise, Oldsmobile.

49B: The Six-Wheel Company, of Philadelphia, Pennsylvania, developed the Safeway 6-wheeled passenger and goods models in 1926. Available with single or dual rear tyres on a Templin bogie, the Model 64 shown here was representative of 1927 production. Power was supplied by a 90-bhp Continental engine.

49C: In 1924 Scania-Vabis constructed a special 'band-driven' postal bus with the front wheels mounted on heavy skis. It was intended for use in the northernmost parts of Sweden where it broke the winter isolation of the Lapland population.

SELDEN

SENTINEL, SHELVOKE & DREWRY

50: Typical of US makes imported into the British Isles to counteract the loss of British passenger models dispatched overseas during World War I was the Selden, designed and constructed at the Rochester, New York, plant of the Selden Motor Vehicle Company. 'PRIDE OF BERKHAMSTED', a charabanc, was owned by Messrs Dwight Bros, of Berkhamsted, Herts.

51A: One of the last steam bus designs was exhibited on a 'Super Sentinel' wagon chassis at the 83rd Royal Show, Leicester, in 1924. 32-seat coachwork was by Messrs E. & H. Hora Ltd, Peckham, South London. Within a year, pneumatic tyres had replaced the solids originally fitted and a more attractive roofline was similarly substituted. Here the machine is seen in its final state.

51B: From 1924 until 1937 over two dozen Shelvoke & Drewry (SD) 'Freighter' passenger models were delivered, the majority to the Tramocar Company, of Brighton, and Crosville Motor Services Ltd. Another operator, however, was the Studland Motor Service Co, of Swanage, Dorset. Shown is one of the 'Mototrams, Chassis No. 4844, supplied on 26 June 1924.

51C: July 1938 saw the delivery of two unique E-Type Shelvoke & Drewry passenger models to Southdown Motor Services Ltd. These were powered by transverse rear engines and were the only machines of this type to be built.

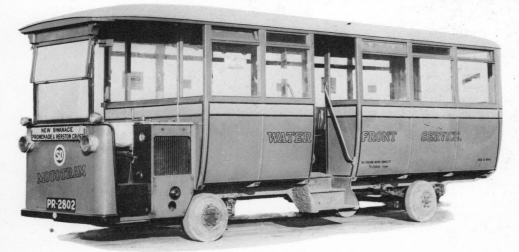

51A   Sentinel

51B   Shelvoke & Drewry

51C   Shelvoke & Drewry

SHEPPEE

SKODA

52 : Sheppee steam wagons, built in Thomas Street, York, from 1905, were noted for their strong resemblance to conventionally-propelled machines. Only two were ever supplied for passenger work, this example being the lightest. The engine was located centrally between the chassis frame sidemembers, with boiler concealed beneath the bonnet.

53A : From 1924 the products of Messrs Laurin & Klement in Czecho-slovakia were known as Skoda. One of the vehicles supplied about this time was a normal-control tractor unit with bus-bodied semi-trailer, intended for short-distance inter-urban work. This model was powered by a 4-cylinder 40-bhp 5.9-litre petrol engine. There were 30 seats and room for 20-25 standing passengers.

53B : In 1928 Skoda introduced this 20-seater model 304N with 4-cyl. 45-bhp engine, supplemented in 1929 by the 6-cyl. 75-bhp Model 306N. Illustrated is a clerestory-roofed design with luggage rack and side access ladder on the former chassis.

53C : The aerodynamically-contoured coachwork mounted on this tandem-drive Skoda of 1939 was constructed as a design exercise and was not intended for general production. The chassis was of rear-engined layout, giving ease of access and a low loading height. The body incorporated an opening roof.

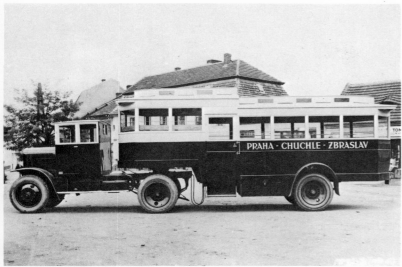

53A   Laurin & Klement/Skoda

53B   Skoda

53C   Skoda

54 : Midland Red introduced its first ON-Series single-deckers in 1934, offered under the SOS marque name. These were powered by a new BMMO 6-litre 6-cylinder petrol engine driving through a 'silent third' transmission. Because of relaxations in restrictions on size it was now possible to make room for 38 persons in each of the Short Bros bodies. Later production carried BMMO radiator badge (Birmingham & Midland Motor Omnibus Co Ltd).

55A : The first front-entrance double-deck models in the Midland Red fleet were based on the SOS FEDD chassis. These made their debut in 1933, a number of batches being delivered up to the outbreak of World War II. The example shown was supplied in 1938, with a 56-seat Brush body.

55B : Last of the SOS ON-Series appeared in 1939. These were designated BMMO Model ONC (for coach) but only a handful were supplied. FHA 424 carried a rare design of Duple body, incorporating a centre entrance and seating for 30 passengers. Note BMMO badge on radiator grille.

55C : Between 1904 and 1931 the Star Motor Co Ltd, Wolverhampton, produced a number of goods and passenger models. Most famous was the Star 'Flyer', a passenger machine for between 20 and 26 seated persons. This 20-seat Model VB4 of 1927 once operated in the Slough and Windsor areas.

55A SOS/BMMO

55B SOS/BMMO

55C Star

STANLEY

STRAKER, STRAKER-SQUIRE, SUNBEAM

56: The famous Stanley steam car was manufactured by the Stanley Motor Carriage Company of Newton, Massachusetts, USA, from 1901. One of the rarer products of this company was the Stanley Steamer 'Mountain Wagon' of c. 1915, based on a heavy motor car chassis but with seating accommodation for a fair-sized party of people.

57A: The only Straker steamers used for passenger work were owned by the Brailes, Shipston-on-Stour & Stratford-on-Avon Steam Omnibus Co Ltd. Delivered about 1903, these featured rubber pad insulation between chassis and body with a steam-heated saloon to combat wintry weather.

57B: On 3 October 1913 Rotherham Corporation inaugurated its railless trolleybus system, using chain-drive Straker-Squire 'cars'. These had conventional solid-tyred wheels with special guide wheels ahead of the steering axle to ensure that each car did not stray too far from existing tram tracks.

57C: The Sunbeam Trolleybus Co Ltd supplied some Model 38 MF2 4-wheelers to Wolverhampton Corporation between 1936 and 1942. These carried a variety of bodies—by Beadle, Roe and Park Royal— seating 54 or 55 passengers. This example was by Park Royal and could easily be mistaken for a postwar design.

57B Straker-Squire

57A Straker

57C Sunbeam

58 : The Clement-Talbot works in Barlby Road, North Kensington, produced a variety of light chassis from 1920 to 1938. This rather unusual model, a 12-seater 'all-weather' coach based on a 30-cwt WO 'Subsidy' chassis, was supplied to the British military authorities in the early Twenties.

59A : This Czech omnibus of 1909 followed closely the lines of Daimler production at that time, and was known as Nesselsdorf. Passenger access was via a central door at the rear and the usual roof luggage rack was provided. Nesselsdorf vehicles were the direct predecessors of the famous Tatra.

59B : Twenty years later the products of this Czechoslovakian manu-facturer included a 4-cylinder 24-bhp light bus known as the Tatra Model 43. Note the unusual front end design, which incorporated a single-piece assembly of rear-hinged bonnet-cum-wings, and the large rear tyres. The engine was air-cooled with horizontally-opposed cylinders.

59C : A tandem-drive model offered by Tatra from 1933 until 1935 was known as the Model 28. It was a well-proportioned machine intended for long-distance operation in under-developed regions. The pronounced 'snout' at the forward end provided a slightly austere appearance. Note the single tyres throughout, popular at this time. The bus had 28 seats and room for 16 standing passengers.

59A Nesselsdorf/Tatra

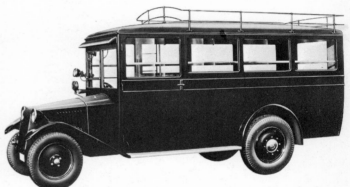

59B Tatra

59C Tatra

THORNYCROFT

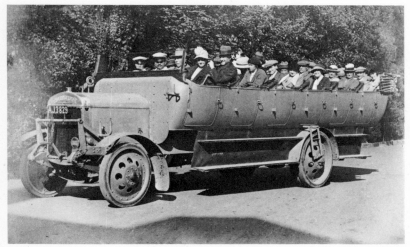

61A   Thornycroft

61B   Thornycroft

60: This 1908 Thornycroft earned the distinction of being the first double-deck bus to negotiate the famous Kirkstone Pass in the North of England.

61A: Thornycroft's J-Type chassis, designed for 'Subsidy' use before and during World War I, was popular after the war as a passenger model. Many were, in fact, reconditioned ex-WD chassis, often fitted with charabanc bodies such as this 24-seater with double running boards.

61B: The Great Western Railway Company operated a considerable fleet of passenger and goods road vehicles, many being based on Thornycroft chassis. This 25-bhp 30-cwt 'Subsidy' model of the Twenties with forward-entrance bus body was photographed at Newport, Mon., Wales.

61C: The 'Boadicea' BC Model was offered in normal- and forward-control layout, powered by a 34-bhp 6-cylinder engine. Isle of Man Road Services operated a small fleet of these, typified by MN 5973 on the front at Douglas c. 1926.

61C   Thornycroft

THORNYCROFT

62A: Forward-control Thornycroft double-deckers could be counted on the fingers of one hand. The SHMD Joint Board ran one or two examples, such as this Hampshire registered model of 1932, but there were no repeat orders.

62B: In South Africa Messrs Thornycroft shared much of the road passenger transportation pioneering work with South African Railways. This was a special version of the 6 x 4 'Amazon', supplied in 1939, which frequently hauled a freight trailer.

62A Thornycroft

62B Thornycroft

63A: An interesting experiment conducted by Messrs Tilling-Stevens Ltd about 1927 was an adaptation of their famous petrol-electric bus chassis, designed to run under its own power or from overhead trolley wires. It was tried in chassis form only on Maidstone Corporation's own trolleybus system but was not generally adopted.

63B: One of the first Volvo buses: a Model LV65 truck chassis with trailing tandem axle and fitted with bodywork by Vagnfabrik Arvika, 1932.

63C: In recent years this German Vomag of *c.* 1925 vintage was discovered in Eire and purchased for preservation. Powered by a 45/50-bhp engine, this machine has a rear-entrance body by Johann Rockinger Wagenfabrik of Munich. The chassis was built by the Vogtländische Maschinenfabrik AG (Vomag) of Plauen-im-Vogtland.

63B Volvo

63A Tilling-Stevens

63C Vomag

INDEX

ACKNOWLEDGEMENTS

This book was compiled and written largely from historic source material in the library of the Olyslager Organisation, and in addition photographs and/or other material was kindly provided or loaned by several individuals and organisations, notably:
H. Brearley
John M. Carpenter
R. T. Coxon
CVRTC Photos
DNM Automotive
M. Dryhurst
Eastern Coachworks
A. Lomas
London Trolleybus Preservation Society
Robert F. Mack
M. R. M. New
and OLD MOTOR.

H46 321 438 5

HAT

Please renew or return items by the date
shown on your receipt

www.hertsdirect.org/libraries

Renewals and   0300 123 4049
enquiries:
Textphone for hearing
or speech impaired   0300 123 4041

Hertfordshire